Anne Wilson

Classic
Essential
~ ❋ ~

Vegetables

KÖNEMANN

~ French Fries ~

Preparation time:
5 minutes
Total cooking time:
20 minutes
Serves 4–6

5–6 large potatoes
oil, for deep-frying

1.~Cut the potatoes lengthways into $1/2$ inch wide sticks. Half-fill a large heavy-based pan with the oil and heat it to hot. Cook the fries in batches for 4–5 minutes, or until pale golden. Remove with tongs or a slotted spoon and drain on paper towels.

2.~Reheat the oil just before serving. Add the fries and cook them for 2–3 minutes, or until golden and crisp; drain on paper towels and serve sprinkled with salt.

NUTRITION PER SERVE (6)
Protein 5 g; Fat 30 g; Carbohydrate 35 g; Dietary Fiber 4 g; Cholesterol 0 mg; 1885 kJ (450 cal)

~ Potato Wedges ~

Preparation time:
10 minutes
Total cooking time:
20 minutes
Serves 4

4–5 large old (brushed) potatoes
1 cup all-purpose flour
3–4 teaspoons chicken seasoning
1 teaspoon white pepper
1 teaspoon sweet

paprika
2 teaspoons garlic powder
oil, for deep-frying
sour cream and sweet chili sauce, for serving

1.~Wash and scrub the potatoes, leaving them wet to help the coating stick. Peel them or leave the skin on, whichever you prefer. Cut each potato into about 10 wedges.
2.~Combine the flour, chicken seasoning, pepper, paprika and garlic powder. Dust the wedges in the seasoned flour. (You can do this by shaking the flour and wedges in a plastic bag.) Reserve the remaining seasoned flour.

3.~Half-fill a large heavy-based pan with the oil and heat it to hot, or heat $3/4$ inch of oil to hot. Deep-fry or shallow-fry the wedges in a few batches for 2–3 minutes each batch, or until pale golden brown. Remove from the pan with tongs or a slotted spoon. Drain on paper towels and allow to cool a little.
4.~Dust with a second coating of seasoned flour, pressing the flour

onto the wedges. Return to the hot oil and cook for another 3–4 minutes, or until the wedges are dark golden and crispy. Remove and drain on paper towels. Sprinkle with a little extra chicken seasoning. Serve the wedges hot with the sour cream and sweet chili sauce for dipping.

NUTRITION PER SERVE
Protein 10 g; Fat 25 g; Carbohydrate 65 g; Dietary Fiber 5 g; Cholesterol 0 mg; 2240 kJ (535 cal)

French Fries (top) and Potato Wedges

~ Ratatouille ~

Preparation time:
20 minutes + standing
Total cooking time:
40 minutes
Serves 4

8 oz eggplant, chopped
1/3 cup olive oil
8 oz zucchini, thickly
  sliced
2 onions, cut in wedges
1 red bell pepper, cubed
1 green bell pepper,
  cubed
2–3 cloves garlic, crushed
1 lb ripe tomatoes,
  chopped

1 ~ Sprinkle the eggplant liberally with salt and leave for 20 minutes. Rinse and dry with paper towels. Heat 3 tablespoons of the oil in a large heavy-based pan. Lightly brown the eggplant and zucchini in batches. Drain on paper towels.

2 ~ Add the remaining oil to the pan. Add the onion and stir over low heat for 2 minutes. Add the peppers and cook for 5 minutes, or until tender but not browned. Add the garlic and chopped tomato and cook, stirring, for about 5 minutes.

3 ~ Stir in the eggplant and zucchini. Simmer for 10–15 minutes to reduce and thicken the sauce. Season with salt and pepper.

NUTRITION PER SERVE
Protein 5 g; Fat 20 g; Carbohydrate 10 g; Dietary Fiber 5 g; Cholesterol 0 mg; 1040 kJ (245 cal)

Place the eggplant in a colander and sprinkle liberally with salt.

Rinse the eggplant well and pat dry with paper towels.

Lightly brown the combined eggplant and zucchini in batches.

Add the peppers to the onion and cook until tender.

～ Asian Greens ～

Preparation time:
5 minutes
Total cooking time:
10 minutes
Serves 4

| 1 lb 10 oz Chinese broccoli (or extra bok choy) | 1 lb baby bok choy |
| 1/3 cup oyster sauce |
| 2 teaspoons sesame oil |

1.～Wash the broccoli and bok choy thoroughly, and shake off the excess water. Trim the ends and roughly chop into large pieces. Cut the bok choy stems in half lengthways if they are very thick.

2.～Place the broccoli pieces in a steamer, preferably bamboo, over a pan of simmering water. Cover and steam for 5–6 minutes. Add the bok choy stems, cover and steam for another 2 minutes.
3.～Transfer the cooked vegetables to a serving bowl. Pour in the oyster sauce and toss gently to coat the bok choy and broccoli. Serve the vegetables drizzled with the sesame oil.

NUTRITION PER SERVE
Protein 15 g; Fat 3 g;
Carbohydrate 10 g; Dietary
Fiber 10 g; Cholesterol 0 mg;
505 kJ (120 cal)

～ Stir-fried Vegetables ～

Preparation time:
15 minutes
Total cooking time:
8 minutes
Serves 4

1 tablespoon sesame seeds	1 clove garlic, crushed
2 green onions	2 teaspoons grated fresh ginger
8 oz broccoli	1 tablespoon soy sauce
1 red bell pepper	1 tablespoon honey
1 yellow bell pepper	1 tablespoon sweet chili sauce
4 3/4 oz baby mushrooms
1 tablespoon oil
1 teaspoon sesame oil

1.～Place the sesame seeds on a baking tray and toast under a broiler until golden. Finely slice the green onions. Cut the broccoli into small florets. Cut the peppers in half, and cut into thin strips. Cut the mushrooms in half.
2.～Heat the oils in a wok or large frying pan. Add the garlic, ginger and green onion. Stir-fry over medium heat for 1 minute. Add the broccoli, pepper and mushrooms. Stir-fry for a further 2 minutes, or until the vegetables are just tender but still bright in color.
3.～Combine the soy sauce, honey and sweet chili sauce in a bowl and mix well. Pour the sauce over the cooked vegetables, and toss lightly to combine. Sprinkle with the toasted sesame seeds.

NUTRITION PER SERVE
Protein 5 g; Fat 10 g;
Carbohydrate 15 g; Dietary
Fiber 5 g; Cholesterol 0 mg;
655 kJ (155 cal)

Asian Greens (top) and Stir-fried Vegetables

∼ Onion Tart ∼

Preparation time:
30 minutes +
35 minutes chilling
Total cooking time:
1 hour 15 minutes
Serves 6

1¼ cups all-purpose
flour
5 oz chilled butter,
chopped
3–4 teaspoons iced water

Filling
2 lb brown onions
1½ oz butter

1 tablespoon olive oil
3 teaspoons all-purpose
flour
3 eggs
¾ cup cream
2 tablespoons milk
pinch of nutmeg
2 oz Gruyère or Swiss
cheese, grated

1 ∼ Sift the flour into a large bowl and add the chopped butter. Using your fingertips, rub the butter into the flour until the mixture resembles fine bread crumbs. Add almost all of the water and use a knife to mix it to a firm dough, adding more water if necessary. Turn the dough out onto a lightly floured surface and gather it together into a ball. (The pastry can also be made in a food processor.)
2 ∼ Wrap the pastry ball in plastic wrap and refrigerate for about 20 minutes. Working quickly, press the chilled pastry into a 10½ inch fluted flan tin. Refrigerate the shell for 15 minutes, or until firm. Preheat the oven to moderate 350°F. Place a sheet of baking paper over the pastry and fill with dried beans or rice. Bake for 10 minutes. Remove the paper and the beans or

rice, and bake the shell for a further 5 minutes, or until the pastry is almost cooked. Allow the shell to cool.
3 ∼ **To make Filling:** Slice the onions into rings. Heat the butter and oil in a large heavy-based pan. Add the onion rings and cook over low heat, stirring occasionally, for 30–35 minutes, or until they are very tender and golden. Sprinkle with the flour and cook, stirring, for 2–3 minutes, or until the mixture is golden. Remove from the heat and allow to cool completely.
4 ∼ Beat the eggs, cream, milk and nutmeg together in a large bowl. Gradually stir in the cooled onion and half the grated cheese. Spoon into the pastry base, sprinkle with the remaining cheese and bake for 20–25 minutes,

or until the tart is golden and cooked through. Set aside for 10 minutes before serving.

NUTRITION PER SERVE
Protein 15 g; Fat 50 g; Carbohydrate 30 g; Dietary Fiber 4 g; Cholesterol 230 mg; 2545 kJ (605 cal)

Note ∼ Brown onions are used in this recipe instead of white onions as they have a higher sugar content. This makes them more suitable for caramelizing and slow cooking. This pastry is very soft and may be difficult to work with in warm weather. Make sure that the butter and water are as cold as possible and work quickly to avoid handling the pastry more than necessary. Working on a marble board or with a fan nearby will make the job easier. Refrigerate the pastry shell until it is firm.

Press the pastry into the tin with lightly floured hands.

Sprinkle the flour over the onion and cook until the mixture is golden.

~ Spaghetti Primavera ~

Preparation time:
20 minutes
Total cooking time:
15 minutes
Serves 4–6

1 lb spaghetti	1 oz butter
1 cup fava beans	7 fl oz cream
6¹/₂ oz sugar snap peas, trimmed	2 oz freshly grated Parmesan
5 oz asparagus	

1 ~ Cook the spaghetti in a large pan of rapidly boiling water until just tender. Drain and return to the pan to keep warm.
2 ~ Boil the beans for 2 minutes. Plunge into iced water, drain and remove the skins. Boil the peas for 2 minutes; plunge into iced water,

then drain. Remove the woody ends from the asparagus and cut into short pieces. Cook in boiling water for 2 minutes, or until bright green and tender. Plunge into iced water; drain.
3 ~ Melt the butter in a heavy-based frying pan. Add the vegetables, cream and Parmesan.

Simmer for 2 minutes, or until heated through; season to taste. Pour the sauce over the pasta and toss to combine.
Note ~ Lima beans can be used instead of fava.

NUTRITION PER SERVE (6)
Protein 15 g; Fat 25 g; Carbohydrate 60 g; Dietary Fiber 5 g; Cholesterol 70 mg; 2245 kJ (535 cal)

Add the spaghetti to a large pan of rapidly boiling water.

Remove and discard the skins from the cooked fava beans.

To remove the woody ends from the asparagus, bend the stem of each spear.

Add the asparagus, fava beans and sugar snap peas to the pan.

～ Mushroom Risotto ～

Preparation time:
20 minutes
Total cooking time:
35–40 minutes
Serves 4–6

3 cups vegetable stock	8 oz arborio rice
1 cup white wine	1/2 cup grated Parmesan
2 oz butter	2 tablespoons chopped
1 tablespoon olive oil	fresh thyme
1 leek, sliced	
8 oz flat mushrooms, sliced	

1～Place the stock and wine in a pan. Bring to the boil, reduce the heat and simmer gently.
2～Heat the butter and oil in a large heavy-based pan. Add the leek and cook over medium heat for 5 minutes. Add the mushrooms and cook for 5 minutes, or until tender. Add the rice and cook, stirring, for 1 minute.
3～Add 1/2 cup of stock and stir until absorbed, then add more stock. Repeat until all the stock has been added and the rice is soft and creamy (about 25–30 minutes). Stir in the Parmesan and thyme, and cook for 1 minute, or until the cheese has melted.

NUTRITION PER SERVE (6)
Protein 10 g; Fat 15 g; Carbohydrate 35 g; Dietary Fiber 4 g; Cholesterol 35 mg; 1430 kJ (340 cal)

Use a kitchen knife to trim and slice the flat mushrooms.

Add the leek to the oil and butter and cook until soft and golden.

Add the rice to the leek and mushrooms and cook, stirring.

Ladle the hot stock and wine into the rice, stirring constantly.

～ Stuffed Potatoes ～

Take hot baked potatoes from the oven, split them open to release the steam, and top with butter and a dollop of sour cream or one of these tasty stuffings for a wholesome meal, hearty snack or stunning side dish.

BAKED POTATOES AND FILLINGS

Preheat the oven to hot 415°F. Scrub 6 large potatoes and pat them dry. Pierce all over with a fork and place directly onto an oven rack and bake for 1 hour, or until tender. Cut a deep cross in the top of each potato and squeeze the corners gently to open. Top with $1/3$ oz butter and a dollop of sour cream. Garnish with chopped chives and black pepper. Alternatively, top with one of the fillings below. Serves 6

NUTRITION PER SERVE
Protein 5 g; Fat 15 g; Carbohydrate 35 g; Dietary Fiber 4 g; Cholesterol 50 mg; 1330 kJ (315 cal)

Garlic Mushroom Topping

Heat 1 oz butter and 1 tablespoon oil in a large frying pan. Add 2 crushed cloves of garlic and 2 sliced green onions; cook over medium heat for 2 minutes, or until the onion is soft. Add $4^3/4$ oz sliced button

mushrooms and cook for 5 minutes, or until the mushrooms are golden brown and tender. Drain off any excess liquid. Fold in 1 tablespoon chopped parsley. Season with salt and pepper. Spoon the topping into the cross-cut baked potatoes. Serves 6

NUTRITION PER SERVE
Protein 5 g; Fat 10 g; Carbohydrate 35 g; Dietary Fiber 5 g; Cholesterol 15 mg; 1025 kJ (245 cal)

Tomato Salsa Topping

Place 6 chopped egg tomatoes, 1 chopped red onion, 1 crushed clove of garlic, 2 tablespoons chopped fresh cilantro and 1 teaspoon olive oil in a bowl and mix to combine. Season to taste with salt and pepper. Divide the filling among the cross-cut potatoes, top with a dollop of sour cream and sprinkle with grated Cheddar cheese. Serves 6

NUTRITION PER SERVE
Protein 10 g; Fat 15 g; Carbohydrate 35 g; Dietary Fiber 5 g; Cholesterol 35 mg; 1290 kJ (305 cal)

Soufflé Potatoes

Preheat the oven to hot 415°F. Slice the tops off 6 large baked potatoes and carefully scoop out the centers, leaving the sides intact. Place the potato in a bowl. Add 1 cup grated Cheddar cheese, 1 cup grated Gruyère cheese, 4 egg yolks and $1/4$ teaspoon dry mustard powder. Season with salt and pepper. Beat 4 egg whites until soft peaks form; fold into the potato mixture. Spoon into the potato shells, place on a baking sheet, and bake for 20–25 minutes, or until the tops are puffed and golden. Serves 6

NUTRITION PER SERVE
Protein 25 g; Fat 20 g; Carbohydrate 35 g; Dietary Fiber 3 g; Cholesterol 165 mg; 1670 kJ (395 cal)

Note～To barbecue the basic potatoes, parboil until they are just tender, wrap in foil and cook until soft.

*Clockwise from top left: a plain Baked Potato
with sour cream and chives; Baked Potato with
Garlic Mushroom Topping; Baked Potato with
Tomato Salsa Topping; Soufflé Potato*

～ Vegetable Tempura ～

Preparation time:
30 minutes
Total cooking time:
15 minutes
Serves 4–6

4 oz broccoli
1 small onion
1 small red bell pepper
1 small green bell pepper
1 carrot
2 oz green beans
light vegetable oil, for
  deep-frying
all-purpose flour, for
  dusting

Batter
1 cup iced water

1 egg yolk
1 cup all-purpose flour,
  sifted

Dipping Sauce
1/4 cup soy sauce
2 tablespoons lemon
  juice
2 tablespoons mirin
  (sweet Japanese wine)
1 tablespoon sake
  (Japanese rice wine)

1. ～Cut the broccoli into small florets, leaving the stalk on. Finely slice the onion, and cut the peppers and the carrot into very thin strips. Cut the beans to the same length, and cut in half lengthways.

2. ～**To make Batter:** Whisk the water and egg yolk in a bowl. Sprinkle the flour over the top and stir in lightly with chopsticks or a fork until just combined. (The mixture will be lumpy.)

3. ～Half-fill a medium heavy-based pan with the oil and heat it to hot. Dust the vegetables in flour, shaking off any excess. Using tongs, gather a small bunch of vegetables (about two pieces of each kind of vegetable) and dip into the batter, pushing any lumps to one side; allow the excess to drain off.

4. ～Carefully lower the bunch of vegetables into the oil. Hold submerged in the oil for a few seconds until the batter begins to set and the vegetables hold together. Release from the tongs and cook until crisp and golden. Drain on paper towels. Repeat until all the vegetables are cooked. Serve immediately with the Dipping Sauce.

5. ～**To make Dipping Sauce:** Place all the ingredients in a bowl and whisk until the sauce is combined.

NUTRITION PER SERVE (6)
Protein 5 g; Fat 20 g; Carbohydrate 20 g; Dietary Fiber 4 g; Cholesterol 30 mg; 1175 kJ (280 cal)

Cut the broccoli into small florets, leaving some of the stalk on.

Mix the batter lightly with chopsticks until just combined.

Using metal tongs, dip bundles of the vegetables into the batter.

Carefully lower the batter-coated vegetables into the oil.

~ Spinach and Feta Pie ~

Preparation time:
30 minutes
Total cooking time:
1 hour
Serves 4–6

2 lb spinach	Parmesan
1/4 cup olive oil	1 cup crumbled feta
1 large onion,	cheese
chopped	1/3 cup ricotta cheese
10 green onions,	4 eggs, lightly beaten
chopped	1 oz butter, melted
1/3 cup chopped fresh	1 tablespoon olive oil,
parsley	extra
1 tablespoon chopped	12 sheets filo pastry
fresh dill	
large pinch of ground	
nutmeg	
1/3 cup freshly grated	

1 Trim any coarse stems from the spinach. Wash the leaves thoroughly and shake off the excess water. Roughly chop the spinach and place it in a large pan. Cover and cook gently over low heat for about 5 minutes, or until the leaves have wilted. (The spinach will gently steam in the water that is left on the leaves. Take care to ensure that the leaves don't catch on the base of the pan and burn.) Drain well and allow the spinach to cool slightly before squeezing it tightly to remove the excess water.
2 Heat the oil in a heavy-based frying pan. Add the onion and cook over low heat for 10 minutes, or until it is very tender and golden. Add the green onion and cook for a further 3 minutes. Remove the pan from the heat. Stir in the drained spinach, parsley, dill, nutmeg,

Parmesan, feta, ricotta and egg. Season with salt and pepper.
3 Preheat the oven to moderate 350°F. Combine the melted butter with the extra oil and use it to grease a 12 x 7 inch baking dish. Lay 4 sheets of filo pastry on top of one another, brushing between each sheet with a little of the oil mixture. Place the layered pastry lengthways in the baking dish. Spread with half of the spinach and cheese mixture. Top with another 4 sheets of the layered filo pastry. Spread with the remaining cheese and spinach mixture and top with the last 4 layered pastry sheets, tucking the pastry into the sides of the dish. Brush the

top with any of the remaining oil and butter mixture. Score the top of the pastry into diamonds with a sharp knife. Bake for 40–45 minutes, or until the top is golden brown. Cut into pieces and serve warm.

NUTRITION PER SERVE (6)
Protein 20 g; Fat 30 g; Carbohydrate 20 g; Dietary Fiber 5 g; Cholesterol 170 mg; 1795 kJ (425 cal)

Note Swiss chard can be used instead of spinach. Use the same quantity and trim the coarse white stems from the Swiss chard leaves. Feta is a salty cheese that should be stored immersed in lightly salted water and kept refrigerated. Rinse the cheese and pat dry before using.

Cook the spinach gently until the leaves have wilted.

Spread half of the spinach and cheese mixture over the pastry.

～ Honey-glazed Carrots ～

Preparation time:
5 minutes
Total cooking time:
5 minutes
Serves 4

2 carrots, sliced diagonally 1 oz butter	2 teaspoons honey chopped fresh chives, to serve

1 ～ Steam the carrots until they are tender.
2 ～ Place the butter and honey in a small pan. Cook over low heat until they are combined.
3 ～ Pour the butter and honey over the carrots and toss to combine.

Sprinkle the chives over the carrots. Serve hot.

NUTRITION PER SERVE
Protein 1 g; Fat 5 g;
Carbohydrate 4 g; Dietary
Fiber 2 g; Cholesterol 20 mg;
310 kJ (75 cal)

Note ～ This dish can also be cooked in the microwave. Place the carrots and 1 tablespoon water in a microwave-safe bowl. Cover and cook on High for 6–8 minutes; drain. Cook the butter and honey in a microwave-safe bowl on High for 45 seconds, or until melted. Stir to combine. Pour over the carrots, toss to coat and sprinkle with the chives.

～ Cauliflower Cheese ～

Preparation time:
10 minutes
Total cooking time:
15 minutes
Serves 4–6

1 lb cauliflower 1 oz butter 3 teaspoons all-purpose flour 1/2 cup milk 1/4 cup cream	1/3 cup grated Cheddar cheese 1/4 teaspoon paprika chopped fresh chives, to serve

1 ～ Cut the cauliflower into large florets and steam or microwave until just tender.
2 ～ Meanwhile, melt the butter in a pan. Stir in the flour and cook for 1 minute. Remove from the heat and gradually stir in the combined milk and cream. Return to the heat and stir continuously over medium heat until the mixture boils and thickens. Remove from the heat and stir in half the grated cheese. Season with salt and pepper, to taste.
3 ～ Spoon the cheese sauce over the cooked cauliflower and sprinkle with the remaining grated cheese. Place under a preheated broiler and cook for 3 minutes, or until the cheese is golden brown. Sprinkle with the paprika and fresh chives before serving.

NUTRITION PER SERVE (6)
Protein 5 g; Fat 10 g;
Carbohydrate 5 g; Dietary
Fiber 2 g; Cholesterol 35 mg;
565 kJ (135 cal)

Honey-glazed Carrots (top) and Cauliflower Cheese

～ Soups ～

Few foods are more comforting than a simple bowl of warming soup served with hot crusty bread and butter. These creamy vegetable soups are delicious sprinkled with fresh herbs and freshly cracked black pepper.

Creamy Squash Soup

Peel and cut 2 lb butternut squash into large pieces. Heat 2 oz butter in a large heavy-based pan. Add 1 chopped onion and cook over low heat for 10 minutes, or until very soft. Add the chopped squash, cover and cook for 10 minutes. Add 4 cups vegetable stock; bring to the boil. Reduce the heat and simmer for 40 minutes, or until the squash is tender. Allow to cool slightly. Purée the soup in batches in a blender or food processor until smooth. Season with salt and pepper, and sprinkle with chopped chives. Delicious served with a dollop of sour cream. Serves 4–6

NUTRITION PER SERVE (6)
Protein 5 g; Fat 15 g; Carbohydrate 15 g; Dietary Fiber 2 g; Cholesterol 50 mg; 960 kJ (230 cal)

Vichyssoise

Heat 2 oz butter in a large heavy-based pan. Add 2 sliced leeks, cover and cook over medium heat for 5 minutes. Add 2 chopped potatoes and 3 cups vegetable stock, and bring to the boil. Reduce the heat and simmer for 20 minutes, or until the potatoes are tender.

Stir in 1 cup cream and season to taste with salt and pepper. Allow to cool slightly. Purée the soup in batches in a blender or food processor until smooth. Serve topped with a sprig of thyme. Serves 4–6

NUTRITION PER SERVE (6)
Protein 4 g; Fat 25 g; Carbohydrate 10 g; Dietary Fiber 4 g; Cholesterol 80 mg; 1255 kJ (300 cal)

Left to right: Creamy Squash Soup; Vichyssoise; Cream of Tomato Soup

Cream of Tomato Soup

Heat 1 tablespoon olive oil in a large heavy-based pan. Add 1 chopped onion and cook for 5 minutes, or until the onion is golden. Add 2 crushed cloves of garlic and cook for 1 minute. Add three 13 oz cans crushed tomatoes, 3 cups vegetable stock, 1 tablespoon tomato paste and 1 tablespoon sugar. Bring to the boil; reduce the heat and

simmer, partially covered, for 20 minutes. Allow the soup to cool slightly. Purée in batches in a blender or food processor until smooth. Return to the pan, stir in 1 cup cream and reheat gently. Season with salt and pepper and sprinkle with chopped fresh herbs. Serves 4–6

NUTRITION PER SERVE (6)
Protein 3 g; Fat 20 g; Carbohydrate 10 g; Dietary Fiber 3 g; Cholesterol 55 mg; 1060 kJ (250 cal)

∼ Eggplant Parmigiana ∼

Preparation time:
45 minutes
Total cooking time:
1 hour 15 minutes
Serves 6–8

2 lb 8 oz very ripe
  tomatoes
¹/₄ cup olive oil
1 onion, diced
2 cloves garlic, finely
  chopped
1 teaspoon salt
2 lb eggplants
oil, for shallow-frying
8 oz bocconcini, sliced

6 oz Cheddar cheese,
  finely grated
1 cup fresh basil leaves,
  roughly torn
¹/₂ cup freshly grated
  Parmesan

1 ∼ Score a cross in the base of each tomato. Cover with boiling water and leave for about 2 minutes. Drain the tomatoes and allow them to cool. Peel the skin in a downwards motion, away from the cross, and discard the skin. To remove the seeds, cut the tomatoes in half horizontally and use a spoon to scoop them out. Chop the tomatoes roughly.

2 ∼ Heat the oil in a large frying pan; add the onion, garlic and salt. Cook over moderate heat until the onion is soft. Add the tomato and simmer for 15 minutes.

3 ∼ Preheat the oven to moderately hot 400°F. Slice the eggplants very thinly and shallow-fry in oil in batches for 3–4 minutes, or until golden brown. Drain on paper towels.

4 ∼ Place one third of the eggplant slices over the base of a 7-cup ovenproof dish. Top with half the bocconcini and Cheddar. Repeat the layers, finishing with a layer of eggplant slices.

5 ∼ Pour the tomato sauce over the eggplant. Scatter the basil leaves over the top. Sprinkle with the Parmesan and bake for 40 minutes. Drain off any excess oil before serving.

NUTRITION PER SERVE (8)
Protein 20 g; Fat 25 g;
Carbohydrate 5 g; Dietary
Fiber 5 g; Cholesterol 50 mg;
1365 kJ (325 cal)

Note ∼ Eggplants tend to absorb a lot of oil during shallow-frying. As an alternative, lightly brush the eggplant with oil and grill until it is golden brown on both sides.

Fry the onion and garlic in the oil, then add the chopped tomato.

Shallow-fry the eggplant in batches, then drain on paper towels.

Arrange layers of eggplant, bocconcini and Cheddar in the dish.

Pour the tomato sauce over the eggplant and sprinkle with the torn basil leaves.

~ Roasted Vegetables ~

Preparation time:
15 minutes
Total cooking time:
1 hour 10 minutes
Serves 6–8

1 lb pumpkin	¼ cup olive oil
1 large sweet potato	1¹/₃ oz butter
8 small onions	

1.~Preheat the oven to moderately hot 400°F. Peel the pumpkin and cut it into large pieces. Peel the sweet potato and cut it into large pieces. Peel the onions, leaving them whole. Pour the oil into a large baking dish and add the butter. Put the baking dish in the preheated oven to heat the oil and butter.

2.~Put the vegetables in the baking dish and turn them or use a pastry brush to coat them with the hot oil and butter. Bake for 45–50 minutes, or until the vegetables are crisp and golden on the outside and cooked through. Turn the vegetables occasionally during cooking to coat with the oil and prevent them sticking.

NUTRITION PER SERVE (8)
Protein 4 g; Fat 10 g; Carbohydrate 15 g; Dietary Fiber 3 g; Cholesterol 15 mg; 720 kJ (170 cal)

Note~A variety of vegetables are suitable for roasting, such as parsnips, turnips, fennel, carrots and garlic cloves.

~ Scalloped Potatoes ~

Preparation time:
20 minutes
Total cooking time:
40 minutes
Serves 4–6

4 potatoes	1¹/₂ cups cream
1 onion	2 teaspoons chicken stock
1 cup grated Cheddar	powder or instant
cheese	bouillon, crushed

1.~Preheat the oven to moderate 350°F. Peel and thinly slice the potatoes. Peel and slice the onion into rings. Arrange a layer of overlapping potato slices in a small baking dish and top with a layer of onion slices. Set aside half of the grated cheese. Sprinkle a little of the remaining cheese on top of the onion. Continue layering in this order until all the potato and onion have been used.

2.~Pour the cream into a small jug. Add the chicken stock powder and whisk gently until combined. Pour the mixture over the layered potato and onion, and sprinkle with the reserved grated cheese. Bake for 40 minutes, or until the potato is tender, the cheese has melted and the top is golden brown.

NUTRITION PER SERVE (6)
Protein 10 g; Fat 35 g; Carbohydrate 15 g; Dietary Fiber 2 g; Cholesterol 105 mg; 1645 kJ (390 cal)

Roasted Vegetables (top) and Scalloped Potatoes

～ Spring Rolls ～

Preparation time:
45 minutes
Total cooking time:
30 minutes
Makes 20

4 dried Chinese mushrooms, or dried porcini	$2^1/3$ oz water chestnuts, chopped
1 tablespoon oil	6 green onions, chopped
2 cloves garlic, crushed	$4^3/4$ oz Chinese or Savoy cabbage, shredded
1 tablespoon grated fresh ginger	1 tablespoon soy sauce
$4^3/4$ oz fried tofu, cut into strips	1 tablespoon all-purpose flour
1 large carrot, cut into fine strips	10 large spring roll wrappers
	oil, for deep-frying

1 Soak the dried mushrooms in hot water for 30 minutes. Drain and squeeze to remove the excess liquid. Slice the mushroom caps and discard the hard stems.

2 Heat the tablespoon of oil in a large wok, swirling gently to coat the base and side. Stir-fry the garlic, ginger, tofu, carrot and water chestnuts for 30 seconds over high heat. Add the green onion and cabbage, and cook for 1 minute, or until the cabbage has just softened. Add the soy sauce and some salt, white pepper and sugar, to taste; cool. Add the sliced mushroom caps.

3 Mix the flour with 2 tablespoons of water to form a paste. Keep the spring roll wrappers covered with a clean damp dish towel while you work. Place two wrappers on a board, one on top of the other. (The rolls are made with two layers of wrappers.) Cut the large square into four squares. Brush the edges of each square with a little flour paste. Place about 1 tablespoon of the filling in the center of one square. With a corner facing you, roll up the wrapper firmly, folding in the sides as you roll. Repeat with the remaining wrappers and filling.

4 Heat the oil in a wok and deep-fry the rolls, about four at a time, for 3 minutes, or until golden. Drain on paper towels.

NUTRITION PER ROLL
Protein 1 g; Fat 4 g; Carbohydrate 3 g; Dietary Fiber 1 g; Cholesterol 0 mg; 200 kJ (45 cal)

Slice the mushroom caps finely, discarding the hard stems.

Place the filling in the center of the square and roll up firmly, folding in the sides.

～ Stuffed Peppers ～

Preparation time:
20 minutes
Total cooking time:
55 minutes
Serves 4

2 large red bell peppers
1/2 cup short-grain rice
1 tablespoon olive oil
1 onion, finely chopped
2 cloves garlic, crushed
1 tomato, finely
    chopped

1 cup grated Cheddar
    cheese
1/4 cup finely grated
    Parmesan
1/4 cup chopped fresh
    basil
1/4 cup chopped fresh
    parsley

1. ～Preheat the oven to moderate 350°F. Slice the peppers in half lengthways. Add the rice to a pan of boiling water and cook for 12 minutes. Drain, and transfer to a bowl.
2. ～Heat the oil in a frying pan, add the onion and cook for 5–8 minutes, or until golden. Add the garlic and cook for 1 minute. Add to the rice with the tomato, cheeses, basil and parsley. Season with salt and pepper.
3. ～Spoon into the pepper shells and place on a baking sheet. Bake for 30 minutes, or until the peppers are soft and the filling is golden brown.

NUTRITION PER SERVE
Protein 15 g; Fat 20 g;
Carbohydrate 25 g; Dietary
Fiber 3 g; Cholesterol 40 mg;
1345 kJ (320 cal)

Cut the peppers in half lengthways, removing the seeds and white membrane.

Add the finely chopped onion and cook until golden.

Mix the onion and garlic into the rice with the tomato, cheese, basil and parsley.

Spoon the rice mixture into the prepared pepper shells.

～ Vegetable Lasagne ～

Preparation time:
40 minutes
Total cooking time:
2 hours 10 minutes
Serves 6

2 large eggplants
6 tablespoons olive oil
2 onions, chopped
3 cloves garlic, crushed
1 medium carrot, finely chopped
1 celery stalk, finely chopped
3¹/₃ oz baby mushrooms, sliced
1 red bell pepper, chopped
1 lb 10¹/₃ oz can crushed tomatoes
2 tablespoons tomato paste
1 cup red wine
1 tablespoon balsamic vinegar

1 tablespoon brown sugar
¹/₄ cup chopped fresh basil
8 oz dried lasagne sheets
11¹/₄ oz spinach, chopped
¹/₂ cup freshly grated Parmesan
¹/₂ cup grated Cheddar cheese

Béchamel Sauce
2 oz butter
¹/₄ cup all-purpose flour
2 cups milk
9²/₃ oz ricotta cheese

1 ～ Slice the eggplants lengthways. Sprinkle with salt and set aside for 20 minutes. Rinse well and pat dry. Brush the eggplant slices lightly with half the olive oil. Cook under a broiler until they are golden brown; drain on paper towels.

2 ～ Heat the remaining oil in a large heavy-based pan. Add the onion and cook over medium heat for 5 minutes, or until soft and golden. Add the garlic, carrot and celery, and cook for 3 minutes. Add the mushrooms and pepper; cook for 3 minutes, or until the mushrooms are tender. Stir in the tomatoes, tomato paste, wine, vinegar and sugar. Bring to the boil; reduce the heat and simmer, uncovered, for 1 hour. Add the basil; set aside.

3 ～ **To make Béchamel Sauce:** Melt the butter in a pan; add the flour. Stir over low heat for 2 minutes, or until the mixture is golden. Remove the pan from the heat and gradually stir in the milk. Return to the heat and bring to the boil, stirring constantly, until the sauce boils and thickens. Simmer for 2 minutes, add the ricotta and stir until smooth. Finally, season with salt and pepper according to taste.

4 ～ Preheat the oven to moderate 350°F. Lightly grease a 12-cup ovenproof dish. Spread a thin layer of vegetable sauce over the base and top with a layer of the lasagne sheets. Build up with a layer of vegetable sauce, spinach, eggplant and Béchamel Sauce. Continue layering in this order, finishing with the Béchamel Sauce. Sprinkle the combined cheeses over the top and bake for 45–50 minutes, or until the lasagne is cooked and the cheese is golden brown. Leave the lasagne for 10 minutes before cutting.

NUTRITION PER SERVE
Protein 25 g; Fat 45 g; Carbohydrate 54 g; Dietary Fiber 10 g; Cholesterol 80 mg; 3080 kJ (730 cal)

Grill the eggplant until golden brown, turning once.

Build up the layers, finishing with the Béchamel Sauce.

∼ Fried Green Tomatoes ∼

Preparation time:
10 minutes
Total cooking time:
20 minutes
Serves 4

1 cup self-rising flour	1 cup buttermilk
2/3 cup cornmeal	6–8 green tomatoes
1 egg, lightly beaten	

1 ∼ Combine the self-rising flour and cornmeal in a bowl. Season with salt and pepper. Place the beaten egg and buttermilk in a separate bowl and whisk to combine.
2 ∼ Cut the tomatoes into 1/2 inch slices. Dip the tomato slices into the egg and buttermilk mixture, then toss in the flour mixture to coat. Shake off any excess flour.
3 ∼ Heat 3/4 inch oil in a large heavy-based frying pan. Cook the tomatoes in batches over high heat until crisp and golden brown on both sides. Drain on paper towels.

NUTRITION PER SERVE
Protein 10 g; Fat 4 g; Carbohydrate 50 g; Dietary Fiber 6 g; Cholesterol 55 mg; 1185 kJ (280 cal)

Note ∼ Stand the cooked tomatoes upright to prevent them from going soggy. Do not overcrowd the pan, or the temperature will drop and the tomatoes will absorb the oil.

Whisk the beaten egg together with the buttermilk.

Cut the tomatoes into slices, about 1/2 inch thick.

Dip the tomatoes into the egg mixture, then toss in the flour mixture to coat.

Fry the coated tomatoes on both sides until golden brown.

~ Fettucine Pomodoro ~

Preparation time:
15 minutes
Total cooking time:
25 minutes
Serves 4–6

3 lb large ripe tomatoes, peeled	1 teaspoon sugar
1 tablespoon olive oil	1 tablespoon chopped fresh oregano
1 onion, chopped	1 tablespoon chopped fresh parsley
2 cloves garlic, crushed	
1 carrot, finely grated	1 tablespoon chopped fresh basil
2 tablespoons tomato paste	1 lb fettucine

1 ~ Score a cross in the base of each tomato. Cover with boiling water and leave for about 2 minutes. Drain the tomatoes and allow them to cool. Peel the skin in a downwards motion, away from the cross, and discard the skin. To remove the seeds, cut the tomatoes in half horizontally and use a spoon to scoop them out. Chop the tomatoes roughly.
2 ~ Heat the oil in a large heavy-based pan. Add the onion and cook for 5 minutes over low heat, or until soft and golden. Add the garlic and cook for 1 minute.

Add the chopped tomato and carrot; cook, stirring occasionally, for 10 minutes. Stir in the tomato paste and sugar. Season with salt and pepper. Bring to the boil and cook for 5 minutes.
3 ~ Cool the mixture slightly and place in a food processor. Process briefly until the sauce reaches the desired consistency. Add all of the chopped herbs and stir to combine. Season with salt and pepper.
4 ~ While the sauce is cooking, add the fettucine to a large pan of rapidly boiling water,

and cook until just tender. Drain and return to the pan. Add the sauce to the pasta and toss well.

NUTRITION PER SERVE (6)
Protein 10 g; Fat 5 g; Carbohydrate 65 g; Dietary Fiber 10 g; Cholesterol 0 mg; 1475 kJ (350 cal)

Note ~ Vine-ripened or plum tomatoes are the most suitable for this recipe. Alternatively, look for cooking tomatoes. These are very ripe tomatoes that are perfect for making a rich tomato sauce.

Score a cross in each tomato and cover with boiling water.

Place the cooled sauce in a food processor and process briefly.

～ Pumpkin Gnocchi ～

Preparation time:
40 minutes
Total cooking time:
1 hour 30 minutes
Serves 4

---

1 lb pumpkin
1¹/2 cups all-purpose
  flour
¹/2 cup freshly grated
  Parmesan
1 egg, beaten

Sage Butter
3¹/3 oz butter
2 tablespoons chopped
  fresh sage

1～Preheat the oven to warm 315°F. Brush a baking sheet with oil or melted butter. Cut the pumpkin into large pieces, leaving the skin on, and place on the prepared sheet. Bake for 1¹/4 hours, or until the pumpkin is very tender. Allow to cool slightly and scrape the flesh from the skin, avoiding any tough or crispy parts. Place the pumpkin in a large mixing bowl and lightly mash it with a fork. Sift the flour into the bowl, add ¹/4 cup of the grated Parmesan and the beaten egg, and season with freshly

ground black pepper. Mix until all the ingredients are well combined. Turn the dough out onto a lightly floured surface and gather together into a rough ball.

2～Divide the dough in half. Using floured hands, roll each half into a sausage about 16 inches long. Cut each length of dough into 16 equal pieces. Form each piece into an oval shape and press firmly with the prongs of a floured fork to make an indentation.

3～Bring a large pan of water to the boil. Cook the gnocchi in batches,

gently lowering them into the water. Cook until the gnocchi rise to the surface, and then for a further 3 minutes. Remove from the pan, drain and keep warm.

4～**To make Sage Butter:** Melt the butter in a small pan. Remove from the heat and stir in the chopped sage.

5～To serve, divide the gnocchi evenly among four bowls. Drizzle with the Sage Butter and sprinkle with the remaining Parmesan.

NUTRITION PER SERVE
Protein 15 g; Fat 25 g; Carbohydrate 40 g; Dietary Fiber 3 g; Cholesterol 125 mg; 1945 kJ (465 cal)

Scrape the cooked pumpkin flesh from the skin, avoiding any tough parts.

Cut each of the lengths of dough into 16 equal pieces.

～ Spicy Vegetable Couscous ～

Preparation time:
30 minutes
Total cooking time:
1 hour
Serves 6

1～Heat the oil in a large pan and add the garlic, chilli, leek and fennel. Cook over medium heat for 10 minutes, or until the leek and fennel are soft and golden brown.

2～Add the cumin, coriander, turmeric, garam masala, sweet potato and parsnip. Cook for 5 minutes, stirring to coat the vegetables with spices.

3～Add the vegetable stock; cover and simmer for 15 minutes. Stir in the zucchini, broccoli, tomato, peppers and chickpeas. Simmer, uncovered, for 30 minutes, or until the

2 tablespoons olive oil	8 oz broccoli, cut into florets
2 cloves garlic, crushed	2 tomatoes, peeled and chopped
1 small red chili, finely chopped	1 large red bell pepper, chopped
1 leek, thinly sliced	13^1/$_2$ oz can chickpeas, drained
2 small fennel bulbs, sliced	2 tablespoons chopped fresh flat-leaf parsley
2 teaspoons ground cumin	2 tablespoons chopped fresh lemon thyme
1 teaspoon ground coriander	
1 teaspoon ground turmeric	*Couscous*
1 teaspoon garam masala	1^1/$_4$ cups instant couscous
11^1/$_4$ oz sweet potato, chopped	1 oz butter
2 parsnips, sliced	1 cup hot vegetable stock
1^1/$_2$ cups vegetable stock	
2 zucchini, thickly sliced	

vegetables are tender. Fold in the chopped fresh herbs and serve on a bed of couscous.

4～**To make Couscous:** Place the couscous in a bowl and add the butter. Pour in the hot vegetable stock and leave to absorb for 5 minutes. Fluff the couscous gently with a fork to separate the grains.

NUTRITION PER SERVE
Protein 15 g; Fat 15 g; Carbohydrate 50 g; Dietary Fiber 10 g; Cholesterol 15 mg; 1545 kJ (365 cal)

Cook the leek and fennel until they are soft and golden brown.

Fluff the couscous gently with a fork to separate the grains.

~ Vegetable Purées ~

Add a few flavors to your favorite vegetables, process
until irresistibly smooth and creamy, and serve piping hot with almost
any food for a simple accompaniment that will be the star of the show.

Parsnip Purée

Add 1 lb of parsnips to
a pan of boiling water
and cook until tender.
Drain them well and
transfer to a food
processor. Melt $1^2/3$ oz
of butter in a frying pan;
add 1 crushed clove of
garlic and cook over
medium heat for
2 minutes, or until
the butter is a nutty
brown color. Add the

butter and garlic to
the food processor with
$1/2$ cup chicken stock
and $1/3$ cup cream;
process until smooth and
creamy. Season with sea
salt and freshly cracked
black pepper.
Serves 4–6

NUTRITION PER SERVE (6)
Protein 2 g; Fat 15 g;
Carbohydrate 10 g; Dietary
Fiber 2 g; Cholesterol 40 mg;
655 kJ (155 cal)

Spiced Sweet Potato Purée

Cook 1 lb of chopped
sweet potatoes in boiling
water until they are
tender; drain and transfer
to a food processor. Melt
$1^2/3$ oz butter in a frying
pan; add 1 teaspoon
each of ground cumin
and garam masala, and
1 finely chopped
onion. Cook the onion
over medium heat

Left to right: Parsnip Purée; Spiced Sweet Potato Purée; Garlic and Potato Purée

for 5 minutes, or until the onion is soft and golden. Add the onion mixture to the food processor with $1/3$ cup of orange juice and $1/2$ cup of cream. Process until smooth and creamy.
Serves 4–6

NUTRITION PER SERVE (6)
Protein 2 g; Fat 15 g; Carbohydrate 15 g; Dietary Fiber 2 g; Cholesterol 50 mg; 900 kJ (215 cal)

Garlic and Potato Purée

Cook 1 lb of chopped potatoes in boiling water until they are tender; drain well. Transfer to a large bowl and mash until they are smooth. Soak 4 slices of white bread in $1/4$ cup water for 5 minutes. Squeeze out any excess moisture. Put the bread in a food processor with 4 crushed cloves of garlic and process until smooth. Add the bread

mixture to the potato and, using a wooden spoon, gradually beat in $1/2$ cup olive oil and 1 tablespoon lemon juice. Season with salt and pepper according to taste. Serves 4–6

NUTRITION PER SERVE (6)
Protein 3 g; Fat 20 g; Carbohydrate 25 g; Dietary Fiber 2 g; Cholesterol 0 mg; 1195 kJ (285 cal)

～ Char-grilled Vegetables ～

Preparation time:
15 minutes
Total cooking time:
15 minutes
Serves 4

2 large red bell peppers	*Dressing*
2 large sweet potatoes, sliced	$^{1}/_{3}$ cup olive oil
6 zucchini, halved lengthways	2 tablespoons balsamic vinegar
4 large mushroom caps, thickly sliced	2 tablespoons chopped fresh rosemary
	3 cloves garlic, crushed

1 ～ Remove the seeds and membrane from the peppers and cut the flesh into thick strips.
2 ～ **To make Dressing:** Put the oil, vinegar, rosemary and garlic in a bowl. Whisk to combine.
3 ～ Heat a char-grill or barbecue plate. Put the peppers, sweet potato, zucchini and mushrooms on the heated plate. Brush with the Dressing and cook for 15 minutes, or until the vegetables are tender. Turn the vegetables occasionally and continue to brush with the Dressing.

NUTRITION PER SERVE
Protein 10 g; Fat 20 g; Carbohydrate 35 g; Dietary Fiber 10 g; Cholesterol 0 mg; 1510 kJ (360 cal)

Note ～ If the char-grill plate is small, cook the vegetables in batches. Cover and keep warm.

Cut the peppers into thick strips, removing the seeds and membrane.

Whisk the Dressing ingredients together in a bowl.

Brush the vegetables with the Dressing while they are cooking.

Turn the vegetables over occasionally during cooking.

∽ Vegetable Curry ∽

Preparation time:
25 minutes
Total cooking time:
30 minutes
Serves 4

2 tablespoons red curry paste	1 red bell pepper, chopped
2 cups coconut milk, unsweetened	3 oz baby corn
4 lime or lemon leaves	4³/4 oz beans, chopped
1 onion, finely chopped	2 tablespoons lime juice
2 potatoes, chopped	2 tablespoons fish sauce
6¹/2 oz pumpkin, roughly chopped	2 tablespoons chopped fresh cilantro
3 zucchini, chopped	1 tablespoon light brown sugar

1∽Combine the curry paste, coconut milk and ¹/2 cup water in a wok or large pan. Bring to boil, stirring occasionally.
2∽Add the leaves and onion; boil for 3 minutes. Add potato and pumpkin and cook for 15 minutes, or until tender. Stir in the pepper, zucchini, corn and beans; simmer for 10 minutes, or until the vegetables are tender.
3∽Add the lime juice, fish sauce, cilantro and sugar; cook for 2 minutes. Serve with rice.

Note∽You can buy fish sauce in Asian groceries.

NUTRITION PER SERVE
Protein 10 g; Fat 5 g; Carbohydrate 25 g; Dietary Fiber 5 g; Cholesterol 0 mg; 825 kJ (195 cal)

Roughly chop the pumpkin, and chop the pepper and zucchini.

Add the lime leaves and onion to the curry paste and coconut milk mixture.

Add the chopped potato and pumpkin, and cook until tender.

Stir in the pepper, zucchini, corn and beans; simmer until tender.

～ Stuffed Mushrooms ～

Preparation time:
25 minutes
Total cooking time:
30 minutes
Serves 6

6 large flat mushrooms	1 tablespoon fresh
3 slices lean bacon	thyme leaves
2 tablespoons oil	2/3 cup freshly grated
1 small onion, finely	Parmesan
chopped	
2 cloves garlic, crushed	
4 slices white bread	

1 ～ Preheat the oven to moderate 350°F. Line a baking sheet with foil and brush with oil or melted butter.

2 ～ Remove the stems from the mushrooms and chop stems finely. Remove the rind from the bacon and discard it. Cut the bacon into thin strips. Heat the oil in a heavy-based frying pan. Add the chopped onion and bacon, and cook over medium heat for 5 minutes, or until golden. Add the chopped mushroom stems and garlic to the pan. Cook over medium heat for 3 minutes, or until soft, stirring occasionally. Transfer the mixture to a bowl and set aside to cool.

3 ～ Remove the crusts from the bread, tear it into pieces and place it in a food processor. Process in short bursts for 20 seconds, or until fluffy crumbs form. Add the bread crumbs, thyme leaves and grated Parmesan to the bowl and stir until well combined. Season with salt and pepper.

4 ～ Place the mushroom caps on the prepared tray and spoon the bread crumb and bacon mixture on top. Bake for 20 minutes, or until the bread crumbs are crisp and golden and the mushrooms are tender. Serve hot.

NUTRITION PER SERVE
Protein 10 g; Fat 15 g; Carbohydrate 10 g; Dietary Fiber 2 g; Cholesterol 20 mg; 850 kJ (200 cal)

Note ～ To clean the mushrooms, simply wipe them gently with a dish towel or soft cloth to remove any dirt. Do not immerse them in water or they will be soggy and lose their flavor. To remove the stem, hold the cap in the palm of your hand and twist the stem gently.

Remove the crusts from the bread, tear it into pieces and place in a food processor.

Spoon the bread crumb mixture onto the mushroom caps.

~ Winter Vegetable Soup ~

Preparation time:
30 minutes
Total cooking time:
55 minutes
Serves 6

1 oz butter
1 large leek, thinly
   sliced
1 clove garlic, crushed
2 parsnips, chopped
1 celeriac, peeled and
   chopped
3 potatoes, chopped

2 carrots, chopped
2 turnips, chopped
6 cups vegetable stock
2 zucchini, sliced
2 tablespoons chopped
   fresh chives

1~Melt the butter in a large heavy-based pan and add the sliced leek. Cover and cook over low heat for 10 minutes, or until the leek is soft and golden.
2~Add the crushed garlic and cook, stirring, for 1 minute. Add the parsnip, celeriac, potato, carrot, turnip and stock, and bring to the boil.
3~Reduce the heat to simmer and cook, partially covered, for 30 minutes, or until the vegetables are just tender. Add the zucchini and continue cooking for 10 minutes, or until all of the vegetables are soft. Stir in the chopped chives and serve.

NUTRITION PER SERVE
Protein 5 g; Fat 5 g; Carbohydrate 25 g; Dietary Fiber 10 g; Cholesterol 15 mg; 705 kJ (165 cal)

Use a sharp knife to trim and peel the celeriac, then chop the flesh.

Cook the leek over low heat until very soft and golden.

Add the chopped vegetables and stock to the pan and bring to the boil.

Partially cover the pan and simmer until the vegetables are just tender.

～ Spinach and Ricotta Cannelloni ～

Preparation time:
45 minutes
Total cooking time:
1 hour 15 minutes
Serves 4–6

2 tablespoons olive oil
1 large onion, finely
chopped
2 cloves garlic, crushed
2 lb spinach, finely
chopped
1 lb 5 oz fresh ricotta
cheese
2 eggs, lightly beaten
1/4 teaspoon freshly
ground nutmeg
8 oz dried cannelloni
tubes
1 cup grated mozzarella
cheese
1/2 cup freshly grated
Parmesan

Tomato Sauce
1 tablespoon olive oil
1 large onion, chopped
2 cloves garlic, crushed
1 lb 10 oz ripe
tomatoes, chopped
1/2 cup white wine
2 tablespoons tomato
paste
1 teaspoon light brown
sugar
2 tablespoons chopped
fresh basil

1. ～Heat the oil in a large heavy-based pan. Add the onion and cook for 3 minutes, or until it is golden. Stir in the garlic and cook for 1 minute. Add the chopped spinach and cook for 2 minutes. Cover the pan and steam for 1–2 minutes, or until the spinach is tender. Allow to cool slightly.

2. ～Transfer the spinach mixture to a colander and squeeze to remove any excess moisture. Combine the spinach with the ricotta, beaten eggs and nutmeg. Season with salt and freshly cracked black pepper. Preheat the oven to moderate 350°F, and lightly grease a large ovenproof dish.

3. ～**To make Tomato Sauce:** Heat the oil in a large frying pan, and add the chopped onion. Cook over low heat for 5 minutes, or until the onion is soft and golden. Add the garlic and cook for 1 minute. Add the tomato, wine, tomato paste, brown sugar and basil. Bring the mixture to the boil; reduce the heat and simmer for 15 minutes.

4. ～Spread one third of the Tomato Sauce over the base of the prepared dish. Spoon about 2–3 tablespoons of the spinach mixture into each cannelloni tube and arrange the cannelloni neatly in the dish. Spoon the remaining Tomato Sauce over the stuffed cannelloni and scatter the mozzarella and Parmesan over the top. Bake for 40–45 minutes, or until the cannelloni is tender and the top is crisp and golden brown.

NUTRITION PER SERVE (6)
Protein 35 g; Fat 35 g; Carbohydrate 40 g; Dietary Fiber 10 g; Cholesterol 140 mg; 2505 kJ (490 cal)

Note. ～This recipe can be made using fresh lasagne sheets instead of the dried cannelloni tubes. Cut the lasagne sheets into small rectangles, place the filling on the edge and roll up tightly to conceal the filling. Place the filled tubes seam-side-down in the baking dish and finish as for the dried cannelloni.

Cover the pan and steam until the spinach is tender.

Use a teaspoon to spoon the filling into the cannelloni tubes.

～ Pickles ～

Pickling is an easy way to preserve vegetables, a method reminiscent of the days when a cook's competence was proven by the rows of colorful pickles lining the pantry shelves and overflowing into the kitchen.

Pickled Beetroot

Cook 8 beetroot in a large pan of boiling water for 20 minutes, or until tender. Drain and set aside to cool. Remove the skin from the beetroot and discard. (You may wish to wear rubber gloves to do this to prevent your hands from staining.) Slice the beetroot and layer in a large warm sterilized jar with 6 sprigs of rosemary, 1 thinly sliced onion and the zest of 1 orange. Leave $3/4$ inch at the top of the jar. Combine 1 cup each of white and malt vinegar with $1/2$ cup sugar in a pan. Stir over low heat until the sugar dissolves. Bring to the boil; simmer for 5 minutes. Allow to cool before pouring over the beetroot. Seal, label and store in a cool dark place.

NUTRITION PER 100 G
Protein 1 g; Fat 0 g;
Carbohydrate 10 g;
Dietary Fiber 2 g;
Cholesterol 0 mg;
235 kJ (55 cal)

Note ～To make zest, cut strips of rind from the orange using a sharp knife. Remove the white pith from the rind and discard. Cut the rind into fine strips. This can also be done with a zester.

Dill Pickles

Cut 1 lb small firm cucumbers into quarters lengthways. Place in a colander and sprinkle with sea salt. Cover with a dry cloth and allow the cucumber

to stand overnight.
Rinse under cold water
and drain thoroughly.
Combine 3 cups white
vinegar, 3 tablespoons
sugar, and 2 tablespoons
each of yellow mustard
seeds, dill seeds and
black peppercorns in a
pan. Bring to the boil;
reduce the heat and
simmer for 5 minutes.
Pack the cucumbers
with 6 sprigs of dill
in a warm sterilized jar.
Pour in the liquid

with the seeds.
Press down gently to
remove any air bubbles.
Seal the jar, label and
store in a cool dark
place for at least
3 weeks before serving,
shaking occasionally.

NUTRITION PER **100** G
Protein 1 g; Fat 0 g;
Carbohydrate 5 g; Dietary
Fiber 1 g; Cholesterol 0 mg;
150 kJ (35 cal)

Note ∼Make sure the
cucumbers are kept
completely covered in
the vinegar solution.

Pickled Onions

Peel 2 lb pickling onions
and rinse under cold
water. Pat them dry and
pack into sterilized
jars. Place 4 cups malt
vinegar, 2 tablespoons
allspice, 2 teaspoons sea
salt, 2 tablespoons black
peppercorns, 6 cloves
and 3 bay leaves in a
pan. Bring to the boil;
reduce the heat and
simmer for 2 minutes.
Allow to cool slightly
before pouring over the
onions. Seal and store in
an airtight container.

NUTRITION PER **100** G
Protein 1 g; Fat 0 g;
Carbohydrate 2 g; Dietary
Fiber 1 g; Cholesterol 0 mg;
85 kJ (20 cal)

Left to right: Pickled Beetroot;
Dill Pickles; Pickled Onions

~ Asparagus Hollandaise ~

Preparation time:
10 minutes
Total cooking time:
10 minutes
Serves 4–6

4 egg yolks
6 oz butter, melted
2 tablespoons lemon
  juice
	¹/₂ teaspoon freshly
	  cracked black pepper
	9³/₄ oz fresh asparagus	

1.~Place the egg yolks in a food processor and process for 20 seconds. With the motor running, add the melted butter in a thin steady stream and process until thick and creamy. Add the lemon juice and pepper, and season with salt.

2.~Cut any thick woody ends from the asparagus and discard. Add the asparagus to a pan of boiling water. Cook for 2–3 minutes, or until the asparagus is bright green and tender. Drain quickly and place on serving plates. Spoon the Hollandaise Sauce over the top.

NUTRITION PER SERVE (6)
Protein 3 g; Fat 30 g; Carbohydrate 1 g; Dietary Fiber 1 g; Cholesterol 200 mg; 1135 kJ (270 cal)

Note.~The Hollandaise may be kept warm in a bowl over a pan of simmering water while the asparagus cooks. Do not overheat it, however, or the sauce will split.

~ Creamed Spinach ~

Preparation time:
5 minutes
Total cooking time:
10 minutes
Serves 4

1 lb spinach 1 onion, finely sliced 1 oz butter ¹/₄ cup cream ¹/₄ teaspoon ground nutmeg	¹/₄ cup grated Cheddar cheese

1.~Wash and roughly chop the spinach.
2.~Heat the butter in a large heavy-based frying pan. Add the onion and cook over medium heat for 5 minutes, or until soft and golden. Add the spinach and cook for 2 minutes, or until the spinach is soft.

3.~Stir in the cream and nutmeg and cook for 2 minutes, or until the spinach is tender and the cream is heated through. Sprinkle with the cheese. Serve hot.

NUTRITION PER SERVE
Protein 5 g; Fat 15 g; Carbohydrate 3 g; Dietary Fiber 4 g; Cholesterol 45 mg; 715 kJ (170 cal)

Note.~For a smoother texture, the Creamed Spinach can be puréed in a food processor. Frozen spinach may be used in this recipe. Ensure that it is completely thawed and all excess moisture is squeezed from it, or lay it out on paper towels and leave it to dry.

Asparagus Hollandaise (top) and Creamed Spinach

~ Vegetable Pilaf ~

Preparation time:
20 minutes
Total cooking time:
30 minutes
Serves 6

2 oz butter
2 medium onions, sliced
2 cloves garlic, crushed
1 large red bell pepper,
    finely chopped
2 cups basmati rice
5 cups vegetable stock
1¹/2 cups peas
kernels from 1 fresh
    corn cob

¹/2 cup grated
    Parmesan
2 tablespoons chopped
    fresh chives
2 tablespoons chopped
    fresh cilantro

1~Melt the butter in a large pan. Add the onion and cook for 5 minutes over low heat, or until soft. Add the garlic and cook for 1 minute.
2~Add the pepper and rice and cook for 3 minutes. Stir in the stock. Bring to the boil, stirring once. Reduce the heat and simmer for 5 minutes, or until most of the liquid is absorbed.
3~Stir in the peas and corn; cover. Cook over low heat for 10 minutes, or until the rice is tender.

Stir in the Parmesan and herbs. Season to taste.

NUTRITION PER SERVE
Protein 15 g; Fat 10 g;
Carbohydrate 65 g; Dietary
Fiber 5 g; Cholesterol 35 mg;
1800 kJ (230 cal)

Use a sharp kitchen knife to cut the kernels from the corn cob.

Add the pepper and rice to the fried onion and garlic.

Stir in the vegetable stock and bring to the boil, stirring once.

Once the stock has boiled, simmer until the liquid is absorbed.

~ Herbed Potato Rösti ~

Preparation time:
20 minutes
Total cooking time:
20 minutes
Serves 6

2 lb potatoes
1 onion
2 tablespoons chopped
  fresh chives
2 tablespoons chopped
  fresh parsley

2 eggs, lightly beaten
1/3 cup all-purpose flour
2 tablespoons olive oil
11/3 oz butter

1 ~ Grate the potatoes and the onion. Rinse the potato and squeeze out any excess moisture.
2 ~ Place the grated potato, onion, fresh chives, fresh parsley, beaten eggs and flour in a bowl and mix well.
3 ~ Heat the oil and butter in a large heavy-based frying pan. Drop heaped tablespoons of the mixture into the pan, and flatten them. Cook 3–4 pancakes at a time over medium heat for 2–3 minutes, or until crisp and golden brown, then turn and brown the other side. Drain on paper towel and keep warm while cooking the remaining mixture. Delicious served with a fresh green salad or for breakfast with crispy bacon strips.

NUTRITION PER SERVE
Protein 5 g; Fat 15 g; Carbohydrate 35 g; Dietary Fiber 4 g; Cholesterol 80 mg; 1175 kJ (280 cal)

Chop the chives and parsley finely to make 2 tablespoons of each.

Rinse the grated potato and squeeze out any excess moisture.

Combine the potato and onion with the chives, parsley, eggs and flour.

Drop heaped tablespoons of the mixture into the hot oil and butter.

~ Pesto Bocconcini Tarts ~

Preparation time:
20 minutes
Total cooking time:
45 minutes
Serves 4

6 small plum tomatoes
6 bocconcini
1 sheet puff pastry
1 egg, lightly beaten

Pesto
1 cup fresh basil leaves
2 cloves garlic, chopped
2 tablespoons pine nuts
1/4 cup freshly grated
Parmesan
1/4 cup olive oil

1 ~ Preheat the oven to moderately hot 400°F. Slice the tomatoes in half lengthways and place them cut-side-up on a non-stick baking sheet. Sprinkle them with sea salt and some freshly cracked black pepper. Bake for 30 minutes, or until the tomatoes are tender; remove and set aside to cool slightly.
2 ~ **To make Pesto:** Place the basil leaves, chopped garlic, pine nuts and grated Parmesan in a food processor. Process until the mixture forms a smooth paste. Gradually add the olive oil with the motor running. Process until combined.
3 ~ Cut each bocconcini in half. Cut the sheet of pastry into quarters. Place a spoonful of pesto in the center of each pastry square and spread with the back of a spoon, leaving a 3/4 inch border.
4 ~ Arrange 3 tomato halves and 3 bocconcini halves decoratively on top of the pesto. Brush the border lightly with the beaten egg. Bake on a non-stick baking sheet for 15 minutes, or until the pastry is puffed and golden and the bocconcini is melted.

NUTRITION PER SERVE
Protein 30 g; Fat 45 g;
Carbohydrate 10 g; Dietary
Fiber 2 g; Cholesterol 105 mg;
2340 kJ (555 cal)

Note ~ Bocconcini is the name given to small fresh mozzarella cheese. It was originally made from buffalo milk, but is now made from cow's milk. Buy bocconcini that are white in color; avoid those that show any sign of yellowing. Store in the whey they are sold in until ready to use.

Cook the seasoned tomato halves until they are tender.

Gradually add the olive oil to the food processor, with the motor running.

Using a sharp kitchen knife, cut each bocconcini in half.

Spread a spoonful of pesto over each pastry square.

～ Index ～

Front cover: Honey-glazed
Carrots; Cauliflower Cheese;
Stir-fried Vegetables; and
Spinach and Feta Pie.